And these words which I command you today

shall be in your heart. You shall teach them diligently

to your children, and shall talk of them when you sit

in your house, when you walk by the way,

and when you lie down, and when you rise up.

DEUTERONOMY 6:6,7

PRESENTED TO

_____

WITH LOVE FROM

_____

DATE

_____

THE BIG 10 FOR LITTLE SAINTS
Helping Children Understand the 10 Commandments

Published by Loyal Kids

A Division of Loyal Publishing Inc.

P.O. Box 1892, Sisters, OR 97759

www.loyalpublishing.com

Printed in Italy

International Standard Book Number: 1-929125-04-6

00 01 02 03 04 05 06 — 10 9 8 7 6 5 4 3 2 1

THE BIG

10

for Little Saints

MATT & LISA JACOBSON

Illustrated by SONYA WILSON

LOYAL KIDS

SISTERS, OREGON

Dear Parent, Grandparent, Relative, or Friend of the Family: The words you are about to read to a young child are the Commandments that Moses was given on Mount Sinai. The responsibility to teach our children lies with us. We wrote this simple volume as a discipleship tool to help us teach our children these most important Laws. We hope you find it helpful too.

On occasion, a Commandment is slightly paraphrased, followed by a short explanation. This approach was chosen to enable young children to quickly grasp the meaning. In some cases, the vocabulary is advanced. We felt it was important not to oversimplify the words of the Commandments in order that a childs knowledge and understanding of the written Word can be expanded.

Hopefully you'll find, as we did, these "discussion starters" will take you on a wonderful journey of inquiry and discovery with your children.

Did you know that God wants us all to obey Him? Even Daddy and Mommy must obey God. When we obey God, we show Him that we love Him. God gave us Laws to help us understand what we must do in order to obey Him. These Laws are called The Ten Commandments and God wants you to learn them too!

1

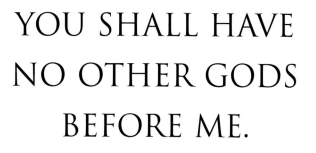

YOU SHALL HAVE NO OTHER GODS BEFORE ME.

God wants you to love Him
more than anything or anybody else.

2

YOU MUST NOT MAKE FOR YOURSELF AN IDOL OF ANY KIND.

God is the only true God and He wants you to worship Him alone. Nothing is more important than God.

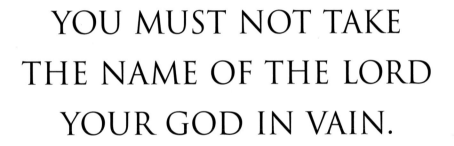

3

YOU MUST NOT TAKE THE NAME OF THE LORD YOUR GOD IN VAIN.

God is holy. We must always speak
His name with reverence and respect.

4

OBSERVE THE SABBATH DAY, TO KEEP IT HOLY.

One day each week, God wants us to rest
and remember the wonderful things
He has done for us.

5

HONOR YOUR FATHER
AND YOUR MOTHER.

God wants you to respect and cheerfully
obey your Daddy and Mommy.

6

YOU MUST NOT MURDER.

God gives life. We must not take away
what He gives.

7

YOU MUST NOT COMMIT ADULTERY.

God wants you to love your husband
or wife all the days of your life.

YOU MUST NOT STEAL.

God says to never take things
that belong to other people.

YOU MUST NOT
TELL A LIE.

God wants you to always tell the truth.

10

YOU MUST NOT COVET THE THINGS THAT OTHER PEOPLE HAVE.

God wants you to be satisfied with
what you have. You must not be envious
of the things that other people have.

These are the Ten Commandments of God.
Let's show that we love God by
obeying His Commandments.

Jesus said that the Ten Commandments
and all the teachings of the Bible
are found in these two laws:

YOU SHALL LOVE THE LORD YOUR GOD WITH ALL YOUR HEART, WITH ALL YOUR SOUL, AND WITH ALL YOUR MIND.

And

YOU SHALL LOVE YOUR NEIGHBOR AS YOURSELF.

And these words which I command you today

shall be in your heart. You shall teach them diligently

to your children, and shall talk of them when you sit

in your house, when you walk by the way,

and when you lie down, and when you rise up.

DEUTERONOMY 6:6,7